GRADE
5

SCHOLASTIC

Success With

Reading Comprehension

New York • Toronto • London • Auckland • Sydney
Mexico City • New Delhi • Hong Kong • Buenos Aires

Teaching *Resources*

State Standards Correlations

To find out how this book helps you meet your state's standards, log on to **www.scholastic.com/ssw**

Scholastic Inc. grants teachers permission to photocopy the reproducible pages from this book for classroom use. No other part of this publication may be reproduced in whole or in part, or stored in a retrieval system, or transmitted in any form or by any means, electronic, mechanical, photocopying, recording, or otherwise without written permission of the publisher. For information regarding permission, write to Scholastic Inc., 557 Broadway, New York, NY 10012.

Written by Linda VanVickle and Kathy Zaun
Cover design by Ka-Yeon Kim-Li
Interior illustrations by Elizabeth Adams
Interior design by Quack & Company

ISBN-13 978-0-545-20080-6
ISBN-10 0-545-20080-6

Copyright © 2002, 2010 Scholastic Inc.
All rights reserved. Printed in the U.S.A.

4 5 6 7 8 9 10   40   17 16 15 14 13 12 11

Introduction

Reading can be fun when high-interest stories are paired with puzzles, interesting facts, and fun activities. Parents and teachers alike will find this book a valuable teaching tool. The purpose of the book is to help students at the fifth grade level improve their reading comprehension skills. They will practice finding the main idea and story details, making inferences, following directions, drawing conclusions, and sequencing. The students are also challenged to develop vocabulary, understand cause and effect, and distinguish between fact and opinion. Practicing and reviewing these important skills will help them become better readers. Take a look at the Table of Contents. Teaching these valuable reading skills to your fifth graders will be a rewarding experience. Remember to praise them for their efforts and successes!

Table of Contents

Terrific Trips

 The **main idea** tells what a story or paragraph is mostly about.

Kelly's friends all sent her letters from their trips. Read each letter. Then circle the main idea of each paragraph.

Dear Kelly,

   Greetings from New York City! Yesterday we visited Central Park, one of the biggest city parks I have ever seen. It is over one-half mile wide and two and one-half miles long with so much to do. We took a carriage ride through the park and even rowed a boat out on one of the park's lakes. My mom loved looking at all the sculptures in the park. Dad enjoyed the free classical music concert in one of the small pavilions. My brother and I liked the zoo most of all. It was small but had some neat animals. Our guide said the Central Park Zoo is the oldest zoo in the United States.

   In the afternoon, we took a ferry to see the famous Statue of Liberty that stands in New York Harbor. Our guide said this 151-foot copper statue was given to the United States by France in 1884 to represent the friendship and freedom both countries share. The tour guide told us that between 1820 and 1937, more than 37 million people came to the United States and were greeted by this statue as they entered our country at Ellis Island. For them it represented the freedom and opportunity they would find in our country. Dad said my own grandparents came to this country through Ellis Island and often spoke of how excited they were to be greeted by "Miss Liberty." Seeing the Statue of Liberty made me so proud of our country and the freedom we have.

   Well, I better run. We are going to try to see a Broadway play. See you soon.

                                          Love,
                                          Christie

1. **Paragraph 1**

    a. **Central Park has activities for visitors of all ages and interests.**

    b. **New York is an incredible city.**

    c. **The Central Park Zoo is the oldest zoo in the United States.**

2. **Paragraph 2**

    a. **The 151-foot Statue of Liberty is impressive.**

    b. **Immigrants came to this country searching for freedom.**

    c. **The Statue of Liberty is a symbol of freedom, opportunity, and friendship.**

Dear Kelly,

   We are having a great time in Washington, D.C. Today we visited two monuments.

   I am sure you have seen pictures of the famous Washington Monument. It is a huge obelisk, over 55 feet in height and covered in white marble. The monument weighs over 90,000 tons! We took an elevator to the top of the monument and had a great view of the whole city of Washington. In the lobby at the base of the obelisk is a large statue of our first president, George Washington. This spectacular monument honors him.

   Next, we visited a very different monument, the Vietnam Veterans Memorial. This monument is two walls of polished black granite arranged in a V-shape. On the walls are carved the names of more than 58,000 men and women who were killed or missing in the Vietnam War. Visitors walk very quietly and respectfully along the granite walls. All along the base of the monument are flowers, flags, and small memorials left by friends and family members. There is so much more we have to see here in Washington, D.C. I'll tell you all about our trip when I get home.

                                    See you soon,
                                    Megan

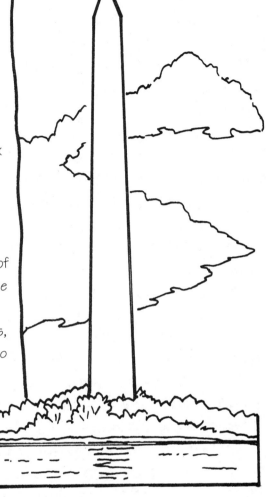

1. **Paragraph 2:**
    a. The Washington Monument honors our nation's first president.
    b. The Washington Monument must have taken a long time to build.
    c. The Washington Monument is a massive, impressive structure.

2. **Paragraph 3:**
    a. Visitors to the Vietnam Veterans Memorial often leave gifts along the granite walls.
    b. A visit to the Vietnam Veterans Memorial is a very moving experience.
    c. The Vietnam Memorial consists of two granite walls arranged in a V-shape.

3. **What is the main idea Megan makes about her visit to these two monuments?**
    a. The two visits to the monuments were very different experiences for her.
    b. Visiting monuments helps her learn about our nation's history.
    a. She is impressed by the different ways monuments are constructed.

Copyright © Scholastic Inc.

Greatest Deal in History

How would you like to buy land at four cents an acre? That is what the United States paid France for the Louisiana Territory in 1803. Many consider this purchase one of the greatest real estate deals in history.

When Thomas Jefferson became president of the United States in 1801, Spain owned the Louisiana Territory and the Floridas. The two countries had treaties that allowed American farmers and merchants to use the shipping ports in these areas. The port of New Orleans was especially important to the American settlers who shipped their products down the rivers that flowed into the Gulf of Mexico. When Jefferson learned that Spain had turned over control of the Louisiana Territory to France, he took action to protect the United States' access to New Orleans. There was also the danger that the French dictator, Napoleon Bonaparte, might try to build an empire in America that would threaten the United States. In 1801, Jefferson sent diplomats to France to negotiate the purchase of New Orleans.

At first Napoleon refused to sell any land to the United States because he did have dreams of expanding his empire. However, the diplomats did not give up, and soon events turned in their favor. French troops in the West Indies had been unable to stop a slave revolt, which forced them to return in defeat to France instead of going on to the Louisiana Territory. Napoleon was also planning a war against Great Britain. Unable to defend the Louisiana Territory and rather than risk losing it to Great Britain or the United States, Napoleon offered to sell the entire territory to the U.S. He could then use the money from the sale to finance his European conquests. On April 30, 1803, a "Treaty of Purchase between the United States and the French Republic" was signed by French and U.S. diplomats. The United States acquired nearly 600 million acres of land for $15 million dollars which calculated to about four cents an acre. While most countries had acquired land through war, the United States achieved its greatest expansion through peaceful negotiations.

Jefferson was rightfully proud of what has become known as the Louisiana Purchase. Acquiring the Louisiana Territory almost doubled the area of the United States. It greatly increased the economic resources in our country and united much of what is now the United States. This bargain buy created all or parts of thirteen states including Louisiana, Arkansas, Missouri, Iowa, North Dakota, South Dakota, Nebraska, Kansas, Wyoming, Minnesota, Oklahoma, Colorado, and Montana. With such expanded land and resources, the United States was poised to become a world power.

Copyright © Scholastic Inc.

Circle the main idea of each paragraph.

1. Paragraph 2:

   a. Spain owned two major territories in North America.

   b. The United States was threatened by French control of the Louisiana Territory.

   c. Thomas Jefferson wanted to purchase only New Orleans.

2. Paragraph 3:

   a. Napoleon would do anything to get money to finance his wars.

   b. U. S. diplomats took two years to negotiate a treaty.

   c. Favorable events and patient diplomacy led to the greatest expansion in United States history.

3. Paragraph 4:

   a. The United States doubled its size with the purchase of the Louisiana Territory.

   b. Thomas Jefferson was proud of the accomplishments of his presidency.

   c. The United States gained many benefits from the Louisiana Purchase.

4. Circle another title for this story.

   What a Great Buy!
   Land for Sale—Cheap, Cheap!

   Napoleon Is Doomed in America
   New States Created

5. Surprisingly, not everyone was happy with the deal the United States made with France to purchase the Louisiana Territory. One Boston newspaper reporter complained that the United States already had enough land and did not need to spend so much money on more. How would you convince this reporter that the United States benefited from this purchase? Write the main benefits of this purchase for the United States.

_____

_____

_____

_____

_____

Read about one of the states which was included in the Louisiana Territory. On another piece of paper, write the main idea of what you read.

Copyright © Scholastic Inc.

A REAL Princess

Details *in a story provide the reader with information about the main idea and help the reader better understand the story.*

Jason and Sam worked all day on their writing assignment. They had to choose a fairy tale and rewrite it. The fairy tale had to be written as if it were a story that could appear in a newspaper today. They decided to use a fairy tale by Hans Christian Andersen. The boys had learned that Hans Christian Andersen was born in Denmark in 1805. He had written a number of fairy tales that made him Denmark's most famous author. His make-believe stories have delighted young children all over the world for many years. Jason and Sam were very pleased with their modern version of the classic fairy tale *The Princess and the Pea*.

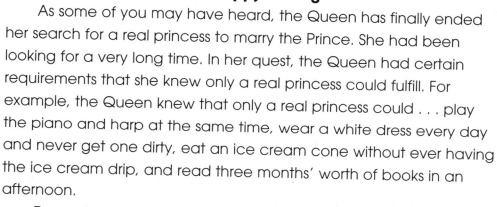

A Happy Ending

As some of you may have heard, the Queen has finally ended her search for a real princess to marry the Prince. She had been looking for a very long time. In her quest, the Queen had certain requirements that she knew only a real princess could fulfill. For example, the Queen knew that only a real princess could . . . play the piano and harp at the same time, wear a white dress every day and never get one dirty, eat an ice cream cone without ever having the ice cream drip, and read three months' worth of books in an afternoon.

Even after searching all over the world, the Queen and the Prince could not find a real princess. They returned home very saddened. However, all hope was not lost! During the terrible storms last Tuesday night, a rain-soaked young woman showed up at the palace, asking for shelter. She claimed she was a princess. To see if the girl spoke the truth about being a princess and to see if indeed she was a real princess, the Queen decided to test her. She hid a pea under 20 mattresses and 20 feather beds. To her delight, the girl slept terribly, for only a real princess can feel a pea beneath all of those mattresses and feather beds.

So, under the most joyous of circumstances, the whole kingdom is invited to the royal wedding of the Prince and his real princess this Saturday at 4:00 P.M. at the palace.

Name _____

1. What was the Queen looking for? _____

_____

2. Circle things a real princess would not do.

    get dirty wearing white   play two instruments at one time

    take three months to read one book   let her ice cream cone drip all
                                           over her

3. Why was the Queen saddened after her search? _____

_____

4. When did the real princess arrive at the palace? Be specific. _____

_____

_____

5. How did the Queen try to determine if the young woman was a real princess? _____

_____

_____

6. Do you think the Queen or the Prince was more concerned about finding a real

princess? Why? _____

_____

_____

7. How do you think the authors of the article feels about the wedding? _____

_____

8. When and where was Hans Christian Andersen born? _____

_____

9. Why did Jason and Sam change the original version of "The Princess and the Pea"?

_____

_____

 **On another piece of paper, design an invitation the Queen could send out for the Prince's
wedding. Include all the details.**

Copyright © Scholastic Inc.

Amazing Animals

All animals are fascinating, and some are truly amazing! For example, did you know that sharks' teeth are as hard as steel, or that kangaroo rats can survive longer without water than camels? Study the chart below to learn more about several amazing animals.

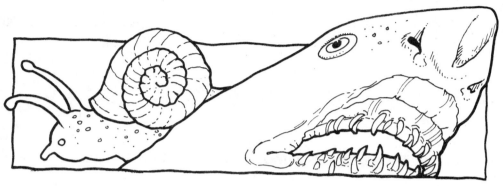

Animal	Where It Lives	Vertebrate or Invertebrate	Fascinating Fact
albatross	near most oceans	vertebrate	can sleep while flying
caterpillar	all over the world	invertebrate	has three times as many muscles as humans
chameleon	forests in Africa and Madagascar	vertebrate	can move its eyes in two different directions at the same time
cockroach	all over the world	invertebrate	can live for up to a week without a head
crocodile	tropical climates	vertebrate	eats only about 50 meals a year
giant squid	oceans throughout the world	invertebrate	has eyes bigger than a human head
giraffe	grasslands in Africa	vertebrate	tallest of animals; has only seven neck bones
penguin	in the southern half of the world with cold ocean waters	vertebrate	eggs kept warm by male until hatched
octopus	oceans throughout the world	invertebrate	has three hearts
shark	oceans throughout the world	vertebrate	never runs out of teeth
snail	almost everywhere—forests, deserts, rivers, ponds, oceans	invertebrate	can sleep for almost three years without waking up
sperm whale	oceans throughout the world	vertebrate	can hold its breath for up to 60 minutes

Copyright © Scholastic Inc.

Name _____

1. Which animal(s) live in the ocean? _____

_____

2. What do the giant squid and the chameleon have in common? _____

_____

3. Which animal would delight the "Tooth Fairy"? _____

_____

4. Label the animals that have backbones with a *V*.

5. Which animals live all, or nearly all, over the world? _____

_____

6. Which animal is very muscular? _____

7. Which animal eats an average of about once a week? _____

8. Which animal can live headless for about a week? _____

9. What is fascinating about a chameleon's eyes? _____

_____

10. Which animal is a "super snoozer"? _____

11. Which animal can hold its breath for nearly an hour? _____

12. Which animal has seven bones in its neck? _____

 Read about another animal. Find a fascinating fact about it to share with your friends.

Copyright © Scholastic Inc.

Name _____

Burger Time

 Context clues *are words or sentences that can help a reader determine the meaning of a new word.*

Reese was **famished**! It was nearly two o'clock, and he had not eaten since breakfast. Reese asked his mom if she would stop at a fast food restaurant on their way home from his baseball game. She rolled her eyes and shook her head. His mother absolutely **loathed** fast food, but with over 300,000 fast food restaurants in the United States, she found it hard to **avoid** them. They were everywhere!

Reese's mother **reluctantly** agreed to **indulge** her son with a fast food lunch, but on the way to the restaurant she tried to explain to Reese the importance of a healthy diet. She had always been a healthy food **fanatic** and knew a lot about foods. She explained to Reese that although fast food is **convenient** to order and very tasty, it often contains **excessive** fat and calories. Reese agreed that a diet of only hamburgers and fries would be unhealthy, and he promised to **definitely** eat a variety of **nutritious** foods as well.

While at the restaurant, Reese's mother began to talk about some of the strange and **unusual** foods eaten by people around the world. In China, for example, some restaurants serve bird's nest soup made from the nests of swallows. Reese was not aware that in Columbia moviegoers may purchase paper cones filled with fried ants as a snack. He was relieved that theaters in the United States served popcorn instead of fried ants. His mother also told him about fugu, a special kind of fish served in Japanese restaurants. If not prepared correctly, fugu can be highly **toxic**. Those who cook it must be specially trained, so the diners do not get sick or die from their meal. Much safer meals included the horse-meat sandwiches served in restaurants in the Netherlands and the grilled guinea pig enjoyed in South American countries. As his mother was explaining how Scottish cooks prepare haggis, a boiled sheep stomach stuffed with oatmeal, Reese began to feel **nauseated** and asked her to please stop talking until he had finished his lunch.

Looking at Reese's pale face, his mother took **pity** on him and promised not to talk about any more strange foods. She did remind him, though, that just because the food was different from what he was used to eating, it was not necessarily bad. In fact, the people in other countries enjoy their food as much as Reese enjoyed fast food. Reese agreed that was probably true, but now all he wanted to enjoy was an ice cream cone for dessert.

Copyright © Scholastic Inc.

1. Use context clues from the story to write each bolded word from the story next to its definition.

    a. sick to one's stomach _____

    b. to give in to the wishes of _____

    c. a devoted person _____

    d. sympathy _____

    e. more than what is acceptable _____

    f. to keep away from _____

    g. unwillingly _____

    h. easy to reach _____

    i. starving _____

    j. certainly _____

    k. healthy _____

    l. disliked intensely _____

    m. poisonous _____

2. Reese's mother loathed fast food. Name two foods that you loathe. _____

    _____

3. What does it mean to say a meal is nutritious? _____

    _____

    _____

4. What are three nutritious foods that you enjoy? _____

    _____

5. Fugu may be toxic if it is not prepared correctly. Would you order fugu in a Japanese

    restaurant? Why or why not? _____

    _____

    _____

 Read about vitamins in a resource book. On another piece of paper, list eight words from the information you read that you do not know. Write a definition for each word using context clues. Then look up each word in a dictionary to see if you are correct.

Copyright © Scholastic Inc.

Terrific Territories

A United States territory is a **region** that belongs to the United States but is not one of the 50 states. It is under the control of the U. S. government. However, it does not have equal status with a state because a territory does not have representation in the national government.

Despite their inequality to the 50 states, all territories are able to govern themselves to a **limited extent**. Their governments are set up by the United States government.

Territorial government is an old **institution**. The first American Territory, the Northwest Territory, was set up in 1787. Until 1867, all territories were created in mainland areas of the United States. However, in 1867, the United States purchased Alaska, and the first territory not directly connected with the rest of the states was **established**. **Gradually**, the United States **acquired** other **distant** territories.

In the past, territories often became states. Alaska and Hawaii were the last two territories that were admitted as states. Currently, the United States has control of about 10 territories. They include Guam, the Virgin Islands, American Samoa, Midway Islands, Wake Island, Johnston Atoll, Baker Island, Howland Island, Jarvis Island, Kingman Reef, Navassa Island, and Palmyra Atoll.

Due to the distance of many of the territories and their experience or inexperience with democratic self-government, the United States does not **extend** the protection and provisions of the Constitution to these areas. Since 1901, the Supreme Court and Congress have classified most territories as either incorporated or unincorporated. Incorporated territories are **entitled** to all rights **guaranteed** by the Constitution. The last two incorporated territories were Alaska and Hawaii. Unincorporated territories are guaranteed only **fundamental** rights.

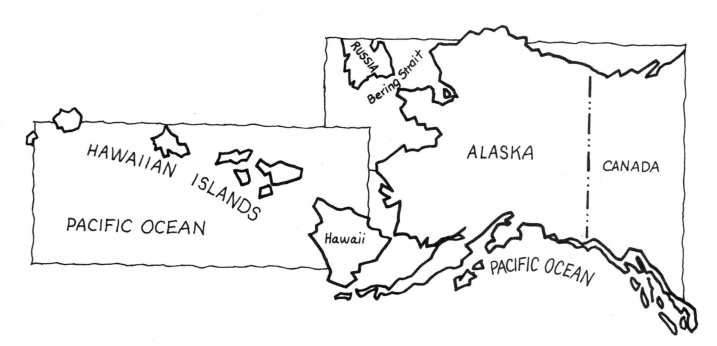

Copyright © Scholastic Inc.

1. Use context clues from the story to help choose the correct definition for each bolded word from the story. Circle the definition.

   a. limited: excessive   restricted   abundant

   b. extent: amount   outside   protection

   c. institution: church   insulating device   established practice

   d. gradually: frequently   currently   over time

   e. acquired: got   ascertained   bought

   f. extend: stretch   offer   make longer

   g. entitled: has the right to   has a desire for   entrusted

   h. guaranteed: protected   licensed   promised

   i. fundamental: basic   inalienable   proper

   j. distant: further   faraway   foreign

   k. status: position   profession   career

   l. region: state   area   country

   m. established: finished   apart   created

2. Label *I* for incorporated or *U* for unincorporated.

   _____ a territory that is guaranteed all rights by the Constitution

   _____ a territory that is guaranteed only basic rights

3. Which territory, purchased by the United States, was the first territory not to be directly connected to the rest of the states? _____

4. Which were the last two territories to become states? _____

Research one of the United States territories. On another piece of paper, list five new words you learned from the article. Then using context clues, write a definition for each word.

Copyright © Scholastic Inc.

Magnificent Musicians

*To **compare** and **contrast** ideas in a passage, a reader determines how the ideas are alike and how they are different.*

Kyle and Cassidy had to write a report together on a famous musician. They had one problem—they could not decide which musician to choose. Kyle wanted to do the report on John Philip Sousa (1854–1932), a famous American composer and bandmaster; Cassidy wanted to do it on Ludwig van Beethoven (1770–1827), a famous German composer.

Kyle was impressed by Beethoven's talent and the fact that his father had taught him to play the violin and piano. However, he favored Sousa because of his ability to write such a wide variety of music. Sousa, who also studied violin, wrote operettas, songs, waltzes, and his famous marches. He is known throughout the world as the "March King." Sousa had the ability to take simple military marches and perk them up with a new and exciting rhythm. Kyle's favorites were *Semper Fidelis* and *The Stars and Stripes Forever*.

Cassidy also liked Sousa's marches and had even performed some dance routines to a couple of them. However, she was impressed with the variety of musical works Beethoven created. She loved to play his symphonies, sonatas, and concertos on the piano. She also liked listening to CD's of this talented composer's work. She especially enjoyed the classical and romantic pieces Beethoven composed, like *Moonlight Sonata*, and the opera *Fidelio*.

Kyle would not have minded focusing on Beethoven because he found him fascinating. He knew that Beethoven began losing his hearing when he was in his twenties and eventually became deaf during the last years of his life. Kyle was intrigued that, through all of his hearing loss, Beethoven continued composing until his death at age 56. However, Kyle preferred to study an American-born composer.

Cassidy felt it did not matter where the composer was born. She admired Beethoven's optimism and faith in moral values, which, she said, came through in his music. She believed that Beethoven helped composers gain the freedom to express themselves. Before his time, composers usually wrote music to teach, to entertain people at social functions, or for religious purposes. Thanks to Beethoven, music became something to enjoy for its own sake.

Cassidy did, however, admire the fact that Sousa made the United States Marine Band one of the finest in the world. He was appointed leader of this band in 1880. Cassidy's father, who had made a career as a marine, said that it was because of this fantastic band that he wanted Cassidy to play an instrument.

So, how were Kyle and Cassidy to decide on whom to write their report? Both musicians were incredibly talented and had a great influence on the world of music. Finally, Cassidy suggested they flip a coin. Heads they would choose Sousa, tails they would choose Beethoven. Kyle tossed the coin high in the air . . .

Copyright © Scholastic Inc.

Name _____

1. Compare and contrast Beethoven and Sousa by writing their descriptions in the diagram. Write the descriptions about Beethoven in the violin and the descriptions about Sousa in the tuba. Write the descriptions about both musicians in the center.

violin	composer	United States Marine Band
German	American	respected worldwide
deaf	1770–1827	*Moonlight Sonata*
marches	*Semper Fidelis*	1854–1932
	influenced music	

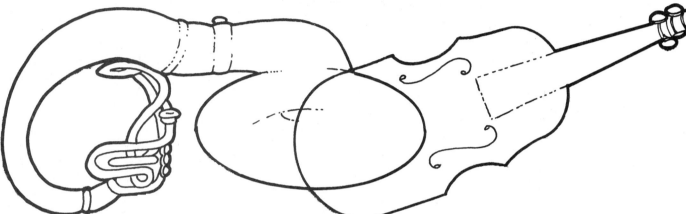

2. List two reasons each student preferred a particular musician.

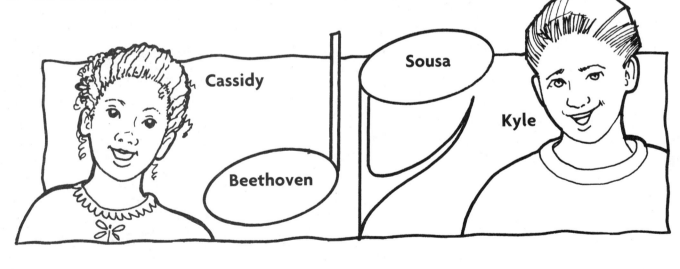

_____   _____

_____   _____

_____   _____

_____   _____

💡 **Read about two other musicians. On another piece of paper, write three similarities and three differences about them.**

Copyright © Scholastic Inc.

Several Cinderellas

When Mrs. Price told her students they were going to read *Cinderella*, they all groaned, saying they already knew that story. Mrs. Price said that they certainly knew one version of *Cinderella*. She explained that *Cinderella* was a folk tale with many different versions found all over the world. She asked the students to search the library to find these different versions of the story. When the students returned to class, they were excited by all the different *Cinderella* stories they found.

Alison told a *Cinderella* story from Ireland. A kind girl has two wicked sisters. After the sisters leave the girl to do all the housework while they go to church, a henwife magically makes beautiful gowns for her as a reward for her kindness. Each Sunday, the girl stands outside the church door wearing a beautiful gown, and everyone admires her beauty. When the people try to talk to her, she rides quickly away on a white horse. At last a prince is able to grab her blue slipper when she rides by. Determined to marry the girl whose foot fits the slipper, the prince travels through the village until he finds her. However, before the prince can marry her, he has to fight all the other men in the village who also want to marry her. The prince wins the fights and marries the girl.

Kara shared a *Cinderella* story from India. In this version a young girl's mother is transformed into a goat. Her father remarries, but the new stepmother is very cruel to the girl and her brother, making them work hard and giving them little food. When the stepmother finds out that the goat is magically providing food for the children, she has the goat killed. Because the goat bones are planted in the ground, the children are still able to magically get food whenever they ask for it. One day when the stepdaughter is washing her face in the river, her nose ring falls into the water. It is eaten by a fish, which is later caught and prepared as a dinner for the king. When the king hears that a nose ring had been found in his fish, he sends word throughout the kingdom that the owner of the ring should come to the palace. The king meets the stepdaughter and marries her because of her beauty and kindness.

Andy then told the Indonesian version of *Cinderella* that he found. In this story the beautiful young girl has a cruel stepmother and stepsister who make her work very hard. One day when the girl is washing clothes in the river, she meets a magic crocodile whom she treats very kindly. Because she is so nice, the crocodile gives her a beautiful silver dress. When the prince comes to the village, looking for a girl to marry, the cruel stepsister takes the dress for herself, leaving the girl only rags to wear. She returns to the crocodile who gives her beautiful golden clothes and slippers and a horse and carriage but warns her to return all the gifts at dawn when the rooster crows. The prince sees the girl dancing in her golden clothes and falls in love. At dawn the girl runs off but loses a golden slipper. The prince searches the village for the girl whose foot will fit into the tiny slipper and, of course, finds her and marries her.

After sharing these stories, the students were surprised to find out that *Cinderella* was such a popular story, told in so many different ways and in so many countries around the world.

Copyright © Scholastic Inc.

Name _____

1. Using the three *Cinderella* versions, complete the following chart. Parts of it have been completed for you.

Country	Family treats girl cruelly.	Girl is beautiful and kind.	Girl has magic helper.	Object proves girl's identity.	There is a happy ending.
Ireland		yes			marries prince
India			goat		
Indonesia	yes			gold slipper	

2. What happens in the *Cinderella* story you knew before reading these versions? Complete the following chart based on the story you know.

Your version of *Cinderella*	Family treats girl cruelly.	Girl is beautiful and kind.	Girl has magic helper.	Object proves girl's identity.	There is a happy ending.

3. What characteristics do all versions of *Cinderella* seem to have in common? _____

_____

_____

_____

4. Where are the biggest differences in the versions? _____

_____

_____

5. How does the Irish *Cinderella* differ in its "happy endings" from the other versions? _____

_____

 On another piece of paper, write your own version of *Cinderella*. Be sure to include all the necessary characteristics, but feel free to make changes in the time and setting and some of the characters. Read your story to a friend.

Copyright © Scholastic Inc.

No Baking Required

Sequencing *is putting the events of a story in the order in which they happen.*

Max was disappointed. He came home from school excited to eat his dad's famous chocolate chip oatmeal cookies. Max had been begging his dad to make them for two weeks. Finally, his dad had a day off, and he told Max he would make the cookies. Wouldn't you know that today, of all days, the oven would not heat up!

Max was craving chocolate. He just had to have some chocolate cookies. Angrily, Max slumped down on the couch and folded his hands across his chest. Max's dad tossed a cookbook to Max. He told Max to quit sulking and start looking through the cookbook. Max's dad told him to look and see if there was anything they could make without using the oven. Max smirked at the idea but thumbed through the cookbook anyway.

What do you know! Max found a chocolate oatmeal cookie recipe that did not need baking! The recipe was called "No-Bake Cookies." Max and his dad decided the recipe was worth a try.

Max and his dad read the recipe together. Then his dad told Max to get out a saucepan. Max's dad got out the necessary ingredients, a big spoon, measuring cups and spoons, and some waxed paper.

Max's dad told him to put ½ cup milk, ¼ cup butter, 4 tablespoons cocoa, and 2 cups of sugar in a pan. Max and he took turns stirring the mixture on the stove until the mixture boiled on medium-high heat for one minute.

Once the hot mixture was pulled off the stove, Max's dad helped him add ½ cup peanut butter, 1 teaspoon of vanilla, and 2 cups of oatmeal. Max stirred. Then Max dropped spoonfuls of the creamy mixture onto waxed paper. Max and his dad could not wait to try these interesting cookies once they had cooled!

The moment arrived. Max and his dad each bit into a "No-Bake Cookie." Delicious! Max was actually kind of glad the oven was broken! Now his dad and he had a new treat to make.

Copyright © Scholastic Inc.

Name _____

1. Number the events in order.

_____ Max got out a saucepan.

_____ Max learned that the oven was broken.

_____ Max and his dad took turns stirring the mixture.

_____ Max was ready to eat some of his dad's chocolate chip oatmeal cookies.

_____ Max and his dad enjoyed a delicious new treat.

_____ Max dropped spoonfuls of the chocolate mixture onto waxed paper.

_____ Max found a "No-Bake Cookie" recipe.

_____ Max thumbed through a cookbook.

2. How are no-bake cookies similar to cookies you bake? _____

_____

3. Number the ingredients in the order in which they are needed.

___ milk   ___ sugar   ___ oatmeal   ___ butter

___ peanut butter   ___ cocoa   ___ vanilla

4. Write words from the story to match each definition.

sad _____

well-known _____

moping _____

wanting badly _____

smiled in a silly way _____

slouched _____

5. Why do you think Max dropped the cookies

onto waxed paper? _____

_____

 On another piece of paper, write the steps in order explaining how to brush your teeth.

Copyright © Scholastic Inc.

Man vs. Machine

 Legends are stories that are told as if they are true. They are set in the real world and are often about a real character. However, the character in a legend is often stronger, smarter, bigger, or better than a real person.

John Henry was an African-American laborer. He is a hero of many American legends in the South. The original story was created when the railroad was greatly expanding in the late 1800s. John Henry symbolized the workers' fight against being replaced by machines. A famous ballad tells how John Henry competed against a steam drill in a race to see whether a man or a machine could dig a railroad fastest. Using only a hammer, John Henry won the race but died of exhaustion. The actual John Henry is said to have died from rock that fell from the tunnel ceiling and crushed him.

The Legend of John Henry

When John Henry was born, the earth shook and lightning struck. He weighed 44 pounds! Shortly after birth, baby John Henry reached for a hammer hanging on the wall. His father knew John Henry was going to be a steel-driving man.

Sure enough, John Henry grew up and worked for the railroad. He was the fastest, strongest steel-driving man in the world. No one could drive more spikes with a hammer than John Henry.

Around 1870, the steam drill was invented. It was said that this machine could dig a hole faster than 20 workers using hammers. A company building a tunnel on one end of a railroad decided to try out the machine. John Henry's company was working on the other end of the tunnel, using men to drill. Both companies bragged and boasted that they were the fastest. Finally, the companies decided to have a race to see which was faster—the steam drill or man. It was John Henry against the steam drill.

Swinging a 20-pound hammer in each hand, John Henry hammered so fast that sparks flew! At the end of the day he had beaten the drill by four feet! That night, John Henry lay down, very proud of his accomplishment, closed his eyes, and never woke up.

1. **Number the events in order.**

   _____ John Henry hammered so hard that sparks flew.

   _____ John Henry was born weighing 44 pounds.

   _____ A company decided to try out the new steam drill.

   _____ They decided to have a race to see if John Henry could beat the steam drill.

   _____ John Henry beat the steam drill and then lay down and died.

   _____ John Henry reached for a hammer hanging on a wall.

   _____ John Henry grew up and became a steel-driving man.

Copyright © Scholastic Inc.

2. Use context clues to find words from "Man vs. Machine" to match each definition. Then write the letters in the matching numbered boxes below to learn an interesting fact about train tracks.

growing ___ ___ ___ ___ ___ ___ ___ ___
         14   25 26 8

first or earliest ___ ___ ___ ___ ___ ___ ___
                   5   11   10   19 13

stood for ___ ___ ___ ___ ___ ___ ___ ___
           4   28   27   17

achievement ___ ___ ___ ___ ___ ___ ___ ___ ___ ___ ___ ___
             12 9   23   2   22 18   1

boasted ___ ___ ___ ___ ___ ___
         20 19   3

great fatigue ___ ___ ___ ___ ___ ___ ___ ___ ___
               24   16   29 15

real ___ ___ ___ ___ ___
      21 6   7

1	2	3	4		W	5	6	7	8		9	10	11	12	13	14
15	16	17		18	19	20	21	2		22	23	20	24			
15	2	25	26		1	0	0		21	27	28	14	29			

3. How is a character in a legend different from a real person? _____
    _____

4. Compare and contrast the death of the legendary John Henry to the death of the

    actual John Henry. _____
    _____
    _____

5. When was the legend of John Henry created? _____
    _____

6. In the end, do you think John Henry really won the race? Explain. _____
    _____
    _____

Copyright © Scholastic Inc.

Talking Too Much

To better understand a character, a reader needs to carefully study or **analyze** a character's personality, qualities, traits, relationships, motivations, and problems.

Parker is such a big talker. He drives David and Andy crazy! Parker thinks he is great at everything. What makes David and Andy even more frustrated with him is the fact that Parker IS good at everything. He always scores goals at soccer games. He scored the most points for the basketball team this year. He won first place overall in the city's swim competition. He always gets hundreds on his spelling tests. He can finish a math test first and get the best score in the class. How can one person be so good at so much?

However, Parker is not good at one thing. He is not good at being a good sport. No matter what Parker does well, he makes sure everyone knows about it. He is also quick to make unkind comments about other kids' mistakes. If David and Andy have to hear about one more goal they could have scored, or one more basket they should have made, or one more test they should have aced, they are going to scream! David and Andy's one wish is that Parker learns to be humble.

Not many people tell Parker what a good job he does or congratulates him on his accomplishments because Parker has already boasted and bragged about them to everyone. He does not give anyone a chance to learn about anything he has done. He is always the first one to tell about his successes. David and Andy sure wish Parker could be more like Ajay.

Ajay is the new kid in class this year. He does not talk much, but he is very good at many sports and is also super smart. It has taken the rest of the kids a while to learn about Ajay and all

of his talents. Andy, David, and the other kids are all happy to congratulate Ajay when he scores a goal or gets a great score on a test. Ajay just smiles and says thanks. He often makes a nice comment back to acknowledge someone's kindness, and he often compliments attempts of others at sporting events or school work. Andy and David have decided they want to learn to act more like Ajay when they experience success. They wish Parker would learn from Ajay, too. Unfortunately, he is busy always patting himself on the back.

Copyright © Scholastic Inc.

1. Write words that describe Parker on his jersey. Write words that describe Ajay on his jersey. Write words that describe both boys on the trophy.

   boastful   unkind   thoughtful   insensitive   humble   intelligent   athletic   kind

2. List two examples of how Parker is not a good sport. _____

   _____

   _____

3. Why do many people usually not compliment Parker on his accomplishments? _____

   _____

   _____

4. Use context clues to find words from the story to match each definition.

   not arrogant   ___ ___ ___ ___ ___ ___

   impolite   ___ ___ ___ ___

   remarks   ___ ___ ___ ___ ___ ___

   aggravated   ___ ___ ___ ___ ___ ___ ___ ___ ___ ___

5. Whom do Andy and David want to be like—Parker or Ajay? Why? _____

   _____

6. Who do you think has more friends—Parker or Ajay? Why? _____

   _____

 Read about a famous athlete or musician. On another piece of paper, write if he or she is a good role model and why.

Copyright © Scholastic Inc.

Peaceful Protesters

Many people in the history of the United States have worked to make this country better by taking a stand against unfair laws and practices. Their peaceful **resistance** to unfair laws and practices brought about positive changes.

Henry David Thoreau, who was born in Concord, Massachusetts, in 1816, always stood up for what he believed to be right. After he graduated from Harvard, Thoreau taught school for a brief time in Concord, but he resigned to **protest** the school's practice of whipping students for misbehavior. Later in his life he was arrested for refusing to pay a poll tax. He refused to pay the tax as a protest against slavery, which was still practiced in the United States, and against the country's involvement in a war against Mexico. Thoreau wrote an essay called "Civil Disobedience" in which he urged people to use peaceful resistance to bring about changes in laws and government policies with which they disagreed. Thoreau's **principles** would **inspire** and influence future protesters like the leaders of the Civil Rights movement.

On December 1, 1955, Rosa Parks, an African-American woman, refused to give up her seat to a white man on a bus in Birmingham, Alabama. At the time, the law said that all African Americans had to sit in the back of public buses. Rosa was arrested for breaking the law. Rosa's simple protest caught the attention of Dr. Martin Luther King, Jr. He and a group of African-American leaders decided to **boycott** the Birmingham buses as a form of peaceful **resistance** to laws that **discriminate** against one group of people. For 368 days African Americans walked or carpooled rather than use the buses. Dr. King was arrested. Threats were made against him and his family, but he and his followers held strong. They continued to boycott the buses and to hold peaceful marches to show their **opposition** to the laws. In 1956, the United States Supreme Court declared Alabama's **segregation** laws unconstitutional. Dr. King's protest was successful! He said, "The strong man is the man who can stand up for his rights and not hit back."

Dr. King's success inspired Cesar Chavez, another believer in peaceful protest. In 1962, he organized farm workers to protest low wages and poor working conditions. Chavez and all the members of the newly organized United Farm Workers of America took a pledge to use only nonviolent methods to bring about change. Through organized protest marches, strikes, and a national boycott of grapes, Chavez and the UFWA were able to improve the lives of the **migrant** farmers. Farm workers earned higher pay and benefits and had safer working conditions. Although Chavez died in 1993, his work continues through the union he founded. In 1994, the Presidential Medal of Freedom, the highest civilian honor in the United States, was awarded **posthumously** to Cesar Chavez. He was the second Mexican American to receive this honor.

Copyright © Scholastic Inc.

Name _____

1. On the bus, write five words that describe these peaceful protesters:

    Henry David Thoreau, Rosa Parks,
    Dr. Martin Luther King, Jr., and Cesar Chavez

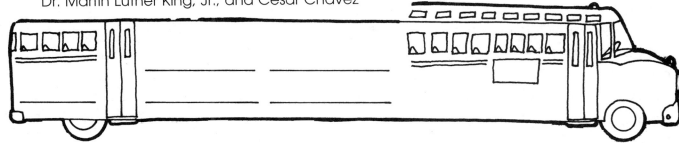

2. Henry David Thoreau, Dr. Martin Luther King, Jr., and Cesar Chavez all believed that one should take a stand against unfair laws and practices. What other belief did they share?

    _____

    _____

3. Complete the puzzle using the bolded words from the story.

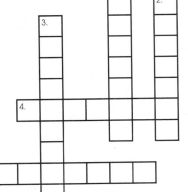

Across
1. after death
4. to object
5. stand against
6. a farm worker who moves from place to place
8. the policy of separating by race

Down
1. basic truths, laws, or beliefs
2. to refuse to buy, sell, or use
3. to show preference in favor of or against
7. to motivate
9. the act of taking a stand against

 On another piece of paper, create an award for another famous African American or one you know and admire. Write why you believe this person deserves the award you created.

Copyright © Scholastic Inc.

Test Time

 Making predictions *is using information from a story to determine what will happen next.*

On Monday, Mrs. Bunch announced to her students that they would have their test covering the 50 states and capitals on Friday. In addition to knowing each state's capital, the students would have to be able to fill in all the states' names on a U.S. map. Mrs. Bunch also told the students to be sure to take special notice of their own state. She even put up a poster in front of the classroom showing the state map along with the state motto and flower. Best friends, Kevin and Matt, both wanted to do well on the test, but each boy studied for the test in a very different way.

Kevin decided to wait until Thursday evening to begin studying. He thought if he learned everything on Thursday, he would be able to remember it better on Friday. After supper on Thursday evening, Kevin took his study notes into the family room so he could watch television while he studied. Mrs. Bunch had given all the students an alphabetical list of the states and their capitals. Kevin read the list over and over again. Then he covered up the capitals and tried to remember what they were as he read each state's name. When he felt that he knew most of the capitals, he then took out his map and began studying where all the states were located. Because Kevin kept taking some time to watch his favorite TV shows, he did not get finished with his studying until very late. The next morning he skipped breakfast so he would not miss his bus and arrive late to school.

Matt, on the other hand, took a different approach to his studying. On Monday evening he made a set of flash cards. On one side of the card, he wrote the name of the state and on the opposite side, he wrote the state's capital. He made one card for each state. He then traced the map of the United States, being careful to outline each state. He took this map to the copy store and made several copies. Now he had some maps on which to practice writing the state names. On Tuesday, Wednesday, and Thursday, Matt spent an hour after supper in his room studying his flash cards and practicing filling in his maps. His mom and dad also helped him by quizzing him about the state capitals while he helped with clearing the table and loading the dishwasher after supper. On his way to school each day, Matt took his flash cards with him on the bus and practiced naming the capitals. Matt went to bed a little earlier on Thursday evening. The next morning he had a good breakfast before catching his bus. On the way to school, he looked over his map and flash cards one last time.

When the boys arrived at school on Friday, they joined their classmates and prepared to take the big test on the states. As Mrs. Bunch handed out the test, Matt noticed that she had taken down the poster of their own state map. Then he received his test and, like his friend Kevin, began to work hard to do his very best.

Copyright © Scholastic Inc.

1. What mistakes do you think Kevin made in the way he studied? _____

_____

_____

_____

2. How was Matt's study plan different from Kevin's?_____

_____

_____

_____

3. The test Mrs. Bunch gave was worth 100 points: one point for naming each state's capital correctly and one point for each state correctly filled in on the map. Write in the number of correct answers you think each boy got on his test.

/100	/100
Kevin	**Matt**

Explain why you think each boy earned the score you wrote. _____

_____

_____

_____

4. Mrs. Bunch included one extra credit question of the test. What do you think it was?

_____

_____

 On another piece of paper, write about a test you thought you were prepared for but it turned out you really were not. Read it to a friend.

Copyright © Scholastic Inc.

The Storm Is Coming

The **cause** is what makes something happen. The **effect** is what happens as a result of the cause.

Haley was so sad. She just couldn't believe it! She was supposed to have her birthday party tomorrow at Super Kool Skateboard Park, but now there was a chance that the city was going to get hit by a hurricane. The party was canceled and would have to be rescheduled. At least Haley's mom had already picked up her birthday cake, so now she could have two cakes.

The meteorologist at the weather center had been keeping a very close eye on Hurricane Dora. This fierce storm originated way out in the Atlantic Ocean near Africa. It was now quickly heading towards the southern part of the United States—somewhere near Miami, which is where Haley lived. The storm had winds of up to 120 miles per hour. This made it a category three hurricane, and Haley knew it could be very damaging. Her city had experienced a number of hurricanes.

So instead of running around with her mom doing last-minute things for her party, Haley was busy helping her mom update their hurricane safety kit. They needed new batteries for the flashlights and radios, fresh water, some canned goods, a new can opener, bread, peanut butter, and any other non-perishable food and drink items Haley could talk her mom into buying. Their kit still had plenty of bandages, blankets, and diapers and baby food for her baby brother. Haley's mom asked Haley to also remind her to get some cash while she was at the store.

While Haley and her mom were busy at the store, Haley's dad was busy at the dock securing their boat. When he finished, he was going to return to the house and cover their windows with plywood that he had already cut for just this kind of emergency.

When all of the preparations are done, Haley's parents will gather their files of important papers, some cherished family photos, and a few clothes for everyone. They will pack everything in their van. Since Haley's grandparents live in Atlanta, Haley and her family will evacuate Miami and go stay with them for a few days. Hopefully, they will all be able to return soon. After all, sometimes winds cause hurricanes to change direction, and they miss their intended target completely. Haley hopes this will happen, but she is also excited that she will get to visit her grandparents.

Copyright © Scholastic Inc.

1. Write *C* for cause or *E* for effect for each pair of sentences.

_____ Haley's birthday party was canceled.

_____ A hurricane was approaching Haley's city.

_____ The meteorologist was watching Hurricane Dora very closely.

_____ Hurricane Dora was a dangerous, category three hurricane.

_____ Haley's dad was prepared for a hurricane.

_____ Haley's dad had plywood already cut for their windows.

2. Match each cause with its effect.

Cause

_____ Haley gets to visit her grandparents.

_____ Winds change their direction.

_____ The storm is very dangerous.

Effect

A. Sometimes hurricanes miss their intended target.

B. Haley's family is evacuating.

C. Haley is excited.

3. List the items Haley's family have in their hurricane safety kit. _____

_____

_____

4. What other items might the family need? Why?

_____

_____

5. Complete the puzzle using words from the story.

Across
1. started
6. treasured
7. make current

Down
2. will not spoil
3. to leave for safety reasons
4. planned; chosen
5. planned again for another time

On another piece of paper, make a list of six items you would take with you if you had to evacuate for safety reasons. Also write a reason why you selected each item.

Copyright © Scholastic Inc.

Awesome Oceans

Making inferences *is figuring out what is happening in a story from clues the author provides.*

Holly's class had been studying world geography for three weeks. However, it was just today that they realized that all four oceans had been visited by various class members. Tori, Kaley, Johnny, and Natalie had each seen one or more of the oceans. Since all of the students lived in Missouri, it was not easy for any of them to travel to a coast.

Holly had never seen an ocean. Someday, though, she wanted to go surfing in one of the three great oceans—the Pacific, the Atlantic, or the Indian. She was afraid the smaller ocean, the Arctic, would be too cold for surfing.

To help the class learn about the world's oceans, Mrs. Steele, the geography teacher, decided to make up a game. She told the four students who had visited one of the oceans to write clues about it on the board. The other students would try to guess which ocean the clues described.

Tori went first. The ocean she had seen was the second largest ocean. It covers about 31,815,000 square miles. Europe and Africa are on its eastern side. However, she had seen it when she was on the east coast of South America. Her dad flies over it when he travels from New York to France for work.

Kaley had seen a very cold ocean. It is the smallest ocean at 5,550,200 square miles. This ocean is located at the top of the world. Kaley and her parents had sailed on this ocean when they visited Canada. Even in the summer, there are big floating ice pieces called floes.

Johnny and Natalie had both seen the largest and deepest ocean in the world. This ocean consists of 64,000,000 square miles. It is so big that it covers about one-third of Earth's surface! Johnny swam and body surfed in it when he went to California last summer to visit his cousins. Natalie used to play in its waves all the time during the two years she and her family lived in Hong Kong. This was the one ocean Holly really wanted to see.

Only Natalie had seen the remaining ocean. This ocean is smaller than the Atlantic by about 6,515,000 square miles. Asia is on the north of this body of water, and Australia and the East Indies lie on the east. Natalie had body surfed in this ocean when she and her family lived in South Africa. Holly decided that one good thing about moving was living in and learning about so many cool places. The other good thing was having so many friends. Natalie had friends all over the world. She was always receiving letters from a lot of interesting places, and she always wrote back.

After all the clues had been given, Mrs. Steele gave each student a map. They were to write the name of each student on the ocean each one had visited. Holly studied her map and the clues on the board. She figured out the answers right away.

Copyright © Scholastic Inc.

Name _____   Making inferences

1. Write the names of the students on the oceans each had visited.

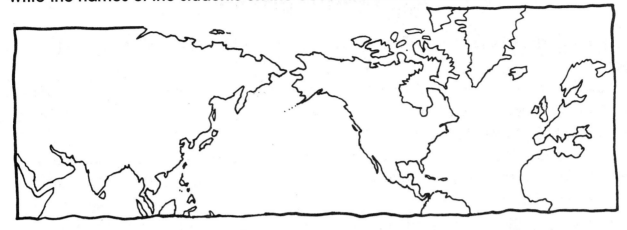

2. Complete the chart by writing each description under the correct ocean.

Africa on east

Asia on north

at top of world

Australia on east

California on east

coldest

covers one-third of
    Earth's surface

deepest

East Indies on east

Europe on east

floes

largest

north of Canada

second largest

South Africa on west

South America on west

Atlantic Ocean	Pacific Ocean	Indian Ocean	Arctic Ocean

 Read about two lakes or other natural landforms. On another piece of paper, write clues about each. Have a friend read the clues and guess what you are writing about.

Copyright © Scholastic Inc.

Green Gift

"Poor Grandma! I wish there was some way we could cheer her up," Amy said to her brother Mark.

Grandma had fallen and broken her leg. The doctor said she would be in a cast for six weeks. Grandma was very active and loved to work in her garden, so she would not enjoy sitting in her chair waiting for her leg to heal.

"I have an idea," said Mark. "I saw some pictures of terrariums in a magazine. Terrariums are little indoor gardens that can be grown in glass jars. Let's make a terrarium for Grandma, so she can enjoy a garden in her house."

Amy thought Mark had a great idea, so the two of them found the magazine article with the directions for making a terrarium and showed their mom. She agreed that a terrarium would be a perfect gift for Grandma. She helped Amy and Mark find a large, clear glass bottle, which they cleaned and checked for leaks. After a trip to the garden shop to buy the materials, they were ready to assemble the terrarium.

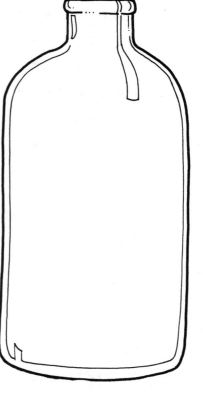

First, they put a small layer of charcoal and gravel drainage material at the bottom of the bottle. This would keep the soil from getting too damp.

Draw a layer of charcoal and gravel at the bottom of the bottle.

Next, they added a layer of dark, rich soil.

Draw a layer of dark soil on top of the drainage materials.

Now they were ready to add the plants. Mark used a long-handled spoon to tap out holes in the soil. Amy had chosen two plants at the garden shop. One was tall with long, thin, green leaves. The other was short with bright pink flowers. Mark placed the plants in the holes and gently tapped the soil down over theirs roots.

Draw the two plants Mark and Amy planted.

To make the terrarium even more colorful, Amy placed some colorful rocks and bright green moss around the plants.

Draw the colorful rocks and green moss that Amy added to the terrarium.

Finally, Mark and Amy lightly watered the plants by pouring water through a small funnel at the top of the bottle. Now the terrarium was ready to take to Grandma.

When Amy and Mark showed Grandma her new terrarium, she was so happy. Now she had a beautiful little garden to enjoy right inside her home.

Copyright © Scholastic Inc.

Name _____

Mark and Amy want to make another terrarium for their Aunt Hilda's birthday, but they lost the magazine article with the directions. Help them make a new set of directions.

1. Make a list of all the materials Mark and Amy needed to assemble the terrarium.

    _____   _____

    _____   _____

    _____   _____

    _____   _____

    _____   _____

2. What must be done to the bottle before adding the materials to it? _____

    _____

3. Tell how to assemble the terrarium. Be sure to use the steps in correct order.

    First, _____

    _____

    Next, add _____

    Now use a long-handled spoon to _____

    and then add_____

    and tap _____

    To make the terrarium more colorful, place _____

    _____

    Finally,_____

    _____

4. Why do you think Amy only chose two plants for the terrarium? _____

    _____

    _____

5. What kinds of plants would not be good choices for a terrarium? _____

    _____

 Cut a label off a product your family is finished using. On another piece of paper, write three questions involving the directions on the label for using the product. Give the label and the questions to a friend to answer.

Copyright © Scholastic Inc.

Sports Galore

 Classifying *means putting similar things into categories.*

Carrie and Ryan were sitting under a tree, thinking about life. Carrie said, "You know, Ryan, I think I am going to be the next Margaret Court Smith. She holds the title for the woman with the most grand slam singles tennis titles. She won 24 titles between 1960 and 1975. I am getting pretty good at tennis. I can pound a pretty hard tennis ball over the net!"

Ryan was not very impressed. "Maybe you can hit the ball hard for a girl. If I wanted to, I could be the next Pete Sampras. Pete holds the title for the most grand slam male singles titles with 13 titles. He won seven Wimbledon titles, four U.S. Open titles, and two Australian Open titles between 1990 and 2000. However, I am saving my talents for the basketball court."

"The basketball court," laughed Carrie. "I am afraid you have a lot of growing to do to catch up with Michael Jordan! This superstar is often called basketball's greatest all-time player. During his career, he averaged 31.5 points per game. He has also been named the NBA's MVP a total of five times!"

"Hey! I will get there—some day! My dad is over six feet tall. It will happen, and then you will be watching me slam dunk a basketball in a nice air-conditioned arena. No hot and humid or stormy weather for me. I like playing sports indoors."

"Well, that's fine," replied Carrie, "but you sure play a lot of football outside. I thought you might want to be the next Emmitt Smith. In 1995, Smith scored a record 25 touchdowns! It only took him six seasons to score 100 career touchdowns. This is the fastest accumulation of touchdowns in NFL history. You know, Ryan, you can toss the football pretty far. Plus, there are lots of indoor stadiums, so your tender body would not have to endure the rain or snow."

"Take it easy, Carrie," said Ryan. "Since you love the cold, I thought you might want to put on your ice skates and be the next Sarah Hughes. I can just see you getting excited when you win the gold medal for figure skating like she did in the 2002 Olympic Games."

"Well, thanks, Ryan," Carrie replied, "but I am not really much of a skater. Actually, I have always wanted to be an architect like my dad."

"Yeah, and I have always wanted to fly airplanes like my mom," said Ryan. The two grew quiet and just sat and thought—some more.

Copyright © Scholastic Inc.

Name _____

1. Write words from the story that fit in each category.

Sports	Sports Equipment
_____	_____
_____	_____
_____	_____
_____	_____

Weather	Famous Sports Figures
_____	_____
_____	_____
_____	_____
_____	_____

2. Write the names of the famous athletes from the story on their matching sports items.

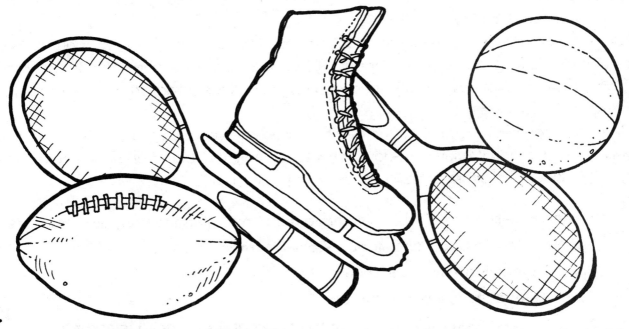

 Read about other famous athletes. Add an athlete's name to each sports item above. On another piece of paper, write one accomplishment each athlete achieved.

Copyright © Scholastic Inc.

A Timely Business

To **draw conclusions** is to use the information in a story to make a logical assumption.

April 15, 1860—The mail did get through! The pony express mail delivery service is happy to announce that its riders finished the first complete run from Saint Joseph, Missouri, to Sacramento, California. It originated on April 3.

For those of you unfamiliar with the pony express, this impressive service employs men who ride fast ponies or horses, relay-style, across a 1,966-mile trail. These men carry letters and small packages. They promise delivery from one end of the trail to the other in 10 days or less!

Finally, there is a way to communicate long distance with friends and acquaintances. You will not have to rely on slow boats or stagecoaches. About 180 riders, 400 fast horses, and 190 pony express stations make up the pony express. Its riders are generally of small build, and many are teenagers. A day's work consists of about a 75-mile trip, with stops at several stations. The stations are about 10 to 15 miles apart. Riders earn about $100 to $150 a month.

Currently, it costs $5.00 to send half an ounce of mail. However, the price could fall to $1.00 in the future if the service continues to do well. Mail usually travels at a rate of about 200 miles a day.

The pony express operates both day and night to ensure timely delivery of important letters and packages. Its riders work in all kinds of weather and even face attacks by Indians. Be kind if you see a hard-working rider.

October 26, 1861—Sad news for the pony express. After operating for only about 19 months, the service closed its doors today. This came just 2 days after the opening of the transcontinental telegraph, a device that has revolutionized long-distance communication. Needless to say, the pony express faces huge monetary losses.

The closing comes just months after the pony express service boasted of a 7-day, 17-hour delivery from St. Joseph, Missouri, to Sacramento, California. The record-breaking ride delivered a copy of President Abraham Lincoln's first address to Congress.

1. **Underline each statement that could have happened after the pony express closed.**

   People relied on boats and stagecoaches for mail delivery.

   Pony express riders had to find new jobs.

   There were many fast horses for sale.

   News traveled more quickly by means of the transcontinental telegraph.

Copyright © Scholastic Inc.

2. How do you think people felt about the pony express closing. _____

_____

_____

3. Circle how you think the pony express riders felt after the pony express closed.

   relieved   sad   defeated   enlightened

4. Underline what you think would have happened to the pony express if it had stayed open after the transcontinental telegraph opened.

   The pony express would have hired more riders.

   People would have stopped using the pony express once they realized how much more efficient it was to communicate over distance by means of the transcontinental telegraph.

   The pony express would have built several more trails for their riders to use.

5. Find words from the story to match each definition. Then circle each word in the puzzle. The words go across, up, down, or backward.

   hires and pays _____

   having a strong impact on _____

   made up of _____

   began _____

   people you know, but not very well _____

   brought about a major change _____

K	A	C	Q	U	A	I	N	T	A	N	C	E	S	C
R	D	L	N	C	T	M	G	O	G	O	Z	R	Y	O
N	E	A	O	M	O	P	N	I	N	E	Y	P	O	N
H	U	C	I	V	E	R	W	Z	U	S	H	S	L	S
O	K	T	Q	N	D	E	I	P	C	O	I	E	P	I
J	S	C	I	U	E	S	M	N	L	P	J	S	M	S
M	A	I	R	E	T	S	F	S	A	I	Y	I	E	T
D	E	Z	I	N	O	I	T	U	L	O	V	E	R	S
R	Q	O	O	R	E	V	O	L	U	T	I	O	N	E
Y	C	U	B	A	D	E	T	A	N	I	G	I	R	O

Railroads were built across the United States in the late 1800s. On another piece of paper, write how you think this changed communication in the United States.

Copyright © Scholastic Inc.

A Super Space Place

The International Space Station (ISS) is being built by thousands of people from 16 countries. All these people are trying to find out if humans can one day live in space.

Floating 230 miles above Earth, the ISS currently looks like a giant building-block project out in space. United States space shuttles and Russian rockets have been transporting tools and pieces of the station into space to help finish building it. From the beginning of its construction in 1998 to its completion, more than 100 major pieces will be assembled to create this amazing space station. When finished, it will be the largest structure ever to float above Earth. The ISS will be larger than a football field and will weigh about one million pounds.

In addition to helping build the space station, the crews are trying to answer such questions as these: How does space travel affect germs? Does the body break down food and nutrients differently in space? Some day, the station may even serve as a launchpad for missions to other planets, such as Mars.

Because of its large size, the ISS needs a lot of power. This power comes from solar energy. To create solar energy, large panels are lined with special materials. These materials collect the sun's energy for power and change the sun's rays into electricity.

So what does it cost to build such a structure? It costs over $60 billion dollars. Although this may seem astronomical, it may be a small price to pay for a project that enables some of the world's finest scientists to work together, exploring space for the world's future.

1. Write *C* for cause or *E* for effect for each pair of sentences.

_____Sixteen countries are building the International Space Station.

_____People want to know if humans can one day live in space.

_____United States space shuttles and Russian rockets carry tools and pieces of the space station into space.

_____The International Space Station, when complete, will be larger than a football field.

_____Panels are lined with special materials that change the sun's rays into electricity.

_____The ISS is powered by solar energy.

Copyright © Scholastic Inc.

2. Write a word from the story to match each definition. Then write each numbered letter on the matching blank below to find out the four most requested foods of astronauts.

constructing ___ ___ ___ ___ ___ ___ ___ ___
            14   13

very great ___ ___ ___ ___ ___ ___ ___ ___ ___ ___ ___
      9   8   3   6

carrying from one ___ ___ ___ ___ ___ ___ ___ ___ ___ ___ ___
place to another   2   5

substances needed for the ___ ___ ___ ___ ___ ___ ___ ___ ___
life and growth of plants, 12   11
animals, or people

having to do with the sun ___ ___ ___ ___ ___
                    1   7

put together ___ ___ ___ ___ ___ ___
                  4   10

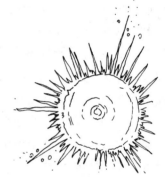

Four most requested foods

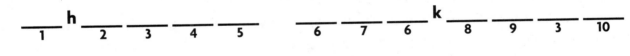

___ h ___ ___ ___ ___   ___ ___ ___ k ___ ___ ___ ___
1 2 3 4 5   6 7 6 8 9 3 10

___ ___ ___ ___ ___ ___ ___ ___
10 11 4 7 12 9 13 11

___ ___ ___ ___ k
1 8 11 9

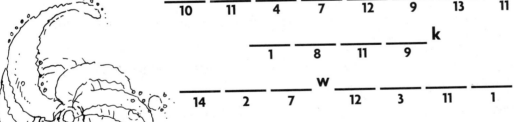

___ ___ ___ w ___ ___ ___ ___
14 2 7 12 3 11 1

3. How does the ISS crew spends its time? _____

_____

4. When finished, how big will the ISS be? _____

_____

5. Why might $60 billion dollars be a small price to pay for the ISS? _____

Copyright © Scholastic Inc.

Brian's Bike

Brian sat on his front doorstep. He really wanted a
new bike. Joe had just gotten one for his birthday, and
Tyler's was only about a year old. Brian had had his for
five years. The seat was up as high as it could go, and his
legs were still too long for his bike. Brian wanted a bike just
like Joe's and Tyler's. Their bikes were perfect for popping
wheelies and cruising over bumps. If only he had $110.00.
All he could come up with was $33.67. Where could he
get the rest of the money he needed?

Brian thought and thought. His birthday was still five
months away, and he was too young to mow lawns. What
could he do to get the money? Maybe his dad would
advance him his allowance for the next few months. He
got three dollars every Friday if he did all of his chores.
His dad had agreed to do this once before, when Brian
needed an extra six dollars. Maybe his sister would loan
him the money. She had a lot of money saved up from baby-sitting. Baby-sitting! That was
it! Brian could baby-sit. Oops! Wait a minute. No one would hire Brian to baby-sit. He still was
not allowed to stay home by himself yet. What could he do to get the money? Brian sat and
thought.

Just then, the phone rang. Mrs. Timmons' dog had gotten out again. She asked Brian if he
could find Fifi for her. Brian said he would be happy to help Mrs. Timmons. She was getting so old.
She could not run after feisty Fifi anymore. Brian immediately started looking for Fifi. He spotted
her behind a tree in the Kirbys' yard.

After chasing Fifi through three different yards, Brian finally caught the frisky dog. He
returned her to Mrs. Timmons. Mrs. Timmons was so
thankful that she handed Brian two dollars. Brian
thanked Mrs. Timmons. He told her that she did not
have to pay him. Then Brian had an idea. Now he
knew what he could do to earn money. He would
set up a pet service! He could take care of people's
pets when they were gone. He figured there were
at least 12 dogs he could look after, a few cats, and
even some fish. Brian would have
that bike in no time!

Copyright © Scholastic Inc.

1. Circle the words that describe Brian.

   lazy   optimistic   industrious   hardworking

   whiney   stressed   ungrateful   pessimistic

2. Why could Brian not baby-sit to earn money? _____

   _____

   _____

3. If Brian's dad agreed to advance him his allowance, how many weeks of allowance

   would Brian need in order to buy his bike? _____

4. If you were Brian's dad, would you advance his allowance for the bike? Why or

   why not? _____

   _____

   _____

5. List Brian's ideas for getting $77.00. Then think of three additional ideas.

   Brian's Ideas   **Other Ideas**

   a.   a.

   b.   b.

   c.   c.

6. What should Brian do to get his pet service started? _____

   _____

   _____

7. How well do you think Brian will do with his new job? _____

   _____

   _____

 Read the want ads in the newspaper. Find a job you would like to have.

Copyright © Scholastic Inc.

From Pole to Pole

 A **fact** is information that can be proven.
(Example: Antarctica is a continent.)

An **opinion** is information that tells what someone thinks.
(Example: The South Pole is the most challenging area to explore.)

Antarctica and the Arctic region are the most southern and northern areas on Earth. These extremely cold areas have been the destinations for many scientific explorations.

Antarctica surrounds the South Pole. It is the coldest of the seven continents. Masses of ice and snow, about one-mile thick, cover most of Antarctica's land. It is the most desolate place on Earth. Few plants can survive in its extreme cold, and its only wildlife lives on the coast.

There is no sunlight at all for months at a time in Antarctica. This keeps the continent very cold. In the winter, temperatures drop below -40°F on the coast and to about -100°F inland. Because it is so cold, little snow falls in this area. The South Pole only gets four-to-six inches of snow each year. However, the existing snow is packed so heavily and tightly that it has formed a great ice cap. This ice cap covers more than 95% of Antarctica.

It is probably not surprising that there are no cities or towns in Antarctica. In fact, no people live there permanently. Since Antarctica was discovered in 1820, many teams of scientists and explorers have braved its cold to learn about this interesting piece of land.

Although very little grows in Antarctica, the seacoast does have a variety of animal life. Whales, seals, penguins, petrels, and fish are among the animals that live in and near Antarctica's coastal waters. All of these animals depend on the sea for food and shelter.

On the opposite end of Earth is the North Pole. This is also a very cold region. It is called the Arctic. It includes the Arctic Ocean and thousands of islands. The northern parts of Europe, Asia, and North America are also part of this region.

Unlike Antarctica, the Arctic is a permanent home for many people. About 90 percent of all Arctic lands are free of snow and ice in the summer—except for Greenland. Although the sun never shines on much of the Arctic during the winter, it does shine on all parts of this area for at least a little while each day from March to September.

As in Antarctica, little plant life can survive in the Arctic. It is plagued not only by cold, but also by wind, a lack of water, and the long, dark winters. Willow trees do grow in the far north of the Arctic but only a few inches high. A permanently frozen layer of soil, called "permafrost," prevents roots from growing deep enough in the ground to properly anchor plants. Therefore, even if plants could survive the cold, they could not grow roots deep enough to enable them to grow very large.

Because it is warmer than Antarctica, the Arctic is home to such animals as reindeer, caribou, bears, and sables. These animals live in pastures all over the Arctic. The seacoast is also home to many birds, including old squaw ducks, eider ducks, falcons, geese, and loons.

Copyright © Scholastic Inc.

1. Write *F* for fact or *O* for opinion.

____ Antarctica is the coldest of all the continents.

____ People do not live in Antarctica because it is too dark without sunshine every day.

____ Farmers would be easily frustrated trying to get things to grow in the Arctic.

____ There are no permanent residents in Antarctica.

____ Antarctica is the most desolate place on Earth.

____ The Arctic includes the northern parts of three continents.

____ People who live in the Arctic enjoy Greenland about 90 percent of the time.

____ Several kinds of animals live in the Arctic.

2. Why do you think people live in the Arctic but not in Antarctica? _____

_____

3. Do you think people will one day live in Antarctica? _____

_____

4. Write *C* for cause or *E* for effect in each pair of sentences.

____ Antarctica is extremely cold.

____ No one lives permanently in Antarctica.

____ "Permafrost" prevents roots from growing very deep in the Arctic.

____ There is a permanently frozen layer of soil called "permafrost" in the Arctic.

5. Circle the main idea of the second paragraph.

Antarctica is the coldest place on Earth.

Antarctica is covered with huge amounts of ice and snow.

Antarctica is a very cold place and cannot support much life.

6. Using context clues from the story, write a definition for each word.

desolate _____

permanent _____

plagued _____

 Read about the continent where you would most like to live. On another piece of paper, list eight reasons you would like to live there. Four reasons should be fact and four opinion.

Copyright © Scholastic Inc.

Loads of Fun

 *Understanding an author's purpose when writing will make appreciating literature easier for the reader. Authors have a purpose when writing, such as to **inform** (give readers facts), to **persuade** (convince readers to do or believe something), or to **entertain** (tell an interesting story).*

June 23

Dear Mom and Dad,

    I am having a great time at camp, but I do miss you both. Yesterday, I went canoeing with my new friends, Taryn and Kari. Boy, did we have a blast! Because it was so hot, we used our paddles to splash each other. We got a little carried away, and our canoe capsized. Unfortunately, our counselor was not amused. The three of us had to mop the mess hall after dinner. Actually, I have become an expert mopper!

    Would it be possible for me to stay at camp another two weeks? Just think, you would have another fourteen days of peace and quiet. This has been such an incredible learning experience. I am certain my school work next year will benefit from the additional camp time. I have already checked with the camp director. She said you just needed to call to verify that I can stay. Guess what? Taryn, Kari, and I can even continue bunking in the same cabin.

    That's it for now. I hear Taryn calling me. The three of us need to meet to plan a prank on another cabin. We have pulled some pretty hysterical pranks!

    Call the camp director as soon as you can.

Love,
Annie

---

1. **What was Annie's purpose for writing this letter?** _____

_____

2. **Do you think Annie's parents will let her stay at camp for two more weeks? Why or why not?** _____

_____

_____

On another piece of paper, change the above letter to show the other two types of an author's purpose.

Copyright © Scholastic Inc.

Page 4
1. a; 2. c

Page 5
1. c; 2. b; 3. a

Pages 6–7
1. b; 2. c; 3. c; 4. What a Great Buy!
5. Answers will vary.

Pages 8–9
1. She was looking for a real princess for the Prince to marry. 2. get dirty wearing white, take three months to read one book, let her ice cream cone drip all over her; 3. She had searched all over the world and had not found a real princess. 4. The real princess showed up at the palace during the terrible storms Tuesday night. 5. She hid a pea under 20 mattresses and 20 feather beds. 6. the Queen, Reasons will vary. 7. The authors feel it is a joyous occasion. 8. Denmark, 1805; 9. They changed it to complete their writing assignment.

Pages 10–11
1. giant squid, octopus, shark, snail, sperm whale; 2. They both have interesting eyes. 3. shark; 4. chameleon, crocodile, shark; 5. albatross, caterpillar, cockroach, giant squid, octopus, shark, snail, sperm whale; 6. caterpillar; 7. crocodile; 8. cockroach; 9. They can move in two directions at the same time. 10. snail; 11. sperm whale; 12. giraffe

Pages 12–13
1. a. nauseated; b. indulge; c. fanatic; d. pity; e. excessive; f. avoid; g. reluctantly; h. convenient; i. famished; j. definitely; k. nutritious; l. loathed; m. toxic; 2.–5. Answers will vary.

Pages 14–15
1. a. restricted; b. amount; c. established practice; d. over time; e. got; f. offer; g. has the right to; h. promised; i. basic; j. faraway; k. position; l. area; m. created; 2. incorporated, unincorporated; 3. Alaska; 4. Alaska and Hawaii

Pages 16–17
1. violin—Beethoven: German, deaf, 1770-1827, *Moonlight Sonata*, piano; tuba—Sousa: United States Marine Band, American, marches, *Semper Fidelis*, 1854-1932, both: violin, composer, respected worldwide, influenced music; 2. Answers will vary.

Pages 18–19
1. Ireland: yes, yes, henwife, blue slipper, marries prince; India: yes, yes, goat, nose ring, marries king; Indonesia: yes, yes, crocodile, gold slipper, marries prince; 2. yes, yes, fairy godmother, glass slipper, marries prince; 3. Family treats girl cruelly. The girl is beautiful and kind. The girl has a magic helper. There is an object that proves the girl's identity. There is a happy ending. 4. the type of magic helper and the object that proves the girl's identity; 5. The prince has to fight all the other men in the village who also want to marry her.

Pages 20–21
1. 5, 2, 6, 1, 8, 7, 4, 3; 2. Answers will vary. 3. milk = 1, sugar = 4, oatmeal = 7, butter = 2, peanut butter = 5, cocoa = 3, vanilla = 6; 4. disappointed, famous, sulking, craving, smirked, slumped; 5. Answers will vary.

Pages 22–23
1. 6, 1, 4, 5, 7, 2, 3; 2. expanding, original, symbolized, accomplishment, bragged, exhaustion, actual, They would circle the earth more than 100 times. 3. He or she is usually stronger, smarter, bigger, or better than a real person. 4. The legendary John Henry died of exhaustion. The actual John Henry died when a rock fell on him. 5. in the late 1800s during the growth of the railroad; 6. Answers will vary.

Pages 24–25
1. Parker—boastful, rude, insensitive; Both—athletic, intelligent; Ajay—humble, kind, thoughtful; 2. He boasts about his accomplishments. He makes comments about other kids' mistakes. 3. He has already boasted and bragged about them to other people. He does not give people a chance to congratulate him. 4. humble, rude, comments, frustrated; 5. Andy and David want to be like Ajay because he is humble about his accomplishments and is kind to others. 6. Answers will vary.

Pages 26–27
1. Answers will vary. 2. They all believed that the protest should be peaceful and non-violent. 3.

Pages 28–29
1. Kevin waited until Thursday to begin studying. He studied while watching television. He stayed up late studying. He skipped breakfast. 2. Matt began studying on Monday. He studied all week for the test. He made several types of review materials. He went to bed early the night before the test. He ate a good breakfast the morning of the test. 3. Answers will vary. 4. Answers will vary. Possible answer: What is the state motto and flower for our state?

Copyright © Scholastic Inc.

Pages 30–31

1. E, C, E, C, C, E; 2. c, a, b;
3. batteries, flashlights, radios, nonperishable food, diapers, baby food, bandages, water, blankets, can opener, canned goods, peanut butter, bread;
4. Answers will vary.
5.

```
o r i g i n a t e d
        o
        n
  e     -           i
  v     p     r     n
  a     e     e     t
c h e r i s h e d   e
  u     i     c     n
  a     s     h     d
  t     h     e     e
  e     a     d     d
        b     u
        l     l
u p d a t e   e
              d
```

Pages 32–33

1. Tori—Atlantic, Kaley—Arctic, Johnny—Pacific, Natalie—Pacific and Indian; 2. Atlantic: Africa on east, Europe on east, second largest, South America on west; Pacific: California on east, covers one-third of Earth's surface, deepest, largest; Indian: Asia on north, Australia on east, East Indies on east, South Africa on west; Arctic: at the top of world, coldest, floes, north of Canada

Pages 34, 35

1. large, clear glass bottle, charcoal, gravel, dark soil, long-handled spoon, plants, colorful rocks, bright green moss, small funnel, water; 2. cleaned and looked for leaks; 3. First, put a small layer of charcoal and gravel drainage material at the bottom of the bottle. Next, add a layer of dark, rich soil. Now use a long-handled spoon to tap out holes in the soil and then add the plants and tap soil over their roots. To make the terrarium colorful, place colorful rocks and bright green moss around the plants. Finally, water the plants by pouring water through a small funnel at the top of the jar. 4. Answers will vary. 5. Answers will vary.

Pages 36–37

1. sports: tennis, basketball, football, figure skating; sports equipment: tennis ball, net, basketball, football, ice skates; weather: hot and humid, stormy, cold, rain, snow; famous sports figures: Margaret Court Smith, Pete Sampras, Michael Jordan, Emmitt Smith, Sarah Hughes; 2. tennis rackets—Margaret Court Smith and Pete Sampras, ice skates—Sarah Hughes, basketball—Michael Jordan, football—Emmitt Smith

Pages 38–39

1. Pony express riders had to find new jobs., There were many fast horses for sale., News traveled more quickly by means of the transcontinental telegraph. 2. Answers will vary. 3. sad, defeated; 4. People would have stopped using the pony express once they realized how much more efficient the transcontinental telegraph was. 5. employs, impressive, consists, originated, acquaintances

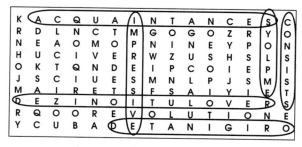

Page 40–41

1. E, C, C, E, C, E;
2. building, astronomical, transporting, nutrients, solar, assembled; four most requested foods of astronauts: shrimp cocktail, lemonade, steak, brownies; 3. building the ISS and conducting experiments; 4. larger than a football field and weighing about one million pounds; 5. because the ISS is a project that allows some of the world's finest scientists to work together, exploring space for the world's future

pages 42–43

1. optimistic, industrious, hardworking;
2. He was too young to baby-sit.
3. 26 weeks; 4. Answers will vary.
5. Brian's Ideas: have Dad advance allowance, borrow money from sister, begin a pet service; Other Ideas: Answers will vary. 6. Answers will vary.
7. Answers will vary.

Pages 44–45

1. F, O, O, F, F, F, O, F; 2. Answers will vary. 3. Answers will vary. 4. C, E, E, C; 5. Antarctica is a very cold place and cannot support much life. 6. Answers will vary.

Page 46

1. to persuade; 2. Answers will vary.

Copyright © Scholastic Inc.